FAR OUT
FABLES

INTRODUCING...

REX

MAMA DUCK

FIRST

SECOND

THIRD

FOURTH

MAMA DINO

THE VELOCIRAPTOR

THE FARM ANIMALS

IN...

Raintree is an imprint of Capstone Global Library Limited, a company incorporated in England and Wales having its registered office at 264 Banbury Road, Oxford, OX2 7DY – Registered company number: 6695582

www.raintree.co.uk
myorders@raintree.co.uk

Designed by Hilary Wacholz
Edited by Abby Huff
Lettered by Jaymes Reed

ISBN 978 1 474 75029 5
21 20 19 18 17
10 9 8 7 6 5 4 3 2 1

British Library Cataloguing in Publication Data: A full catalogue record for this book is available from the British Library.

Printed and bound in China.

FAR OUT FABLES

THE UGLY DINO HATCHLING

A GRAPHIC NOVEL

BY STEPHANIE PETERS
ILLUSTRATED BY OTIS FRAMPTON

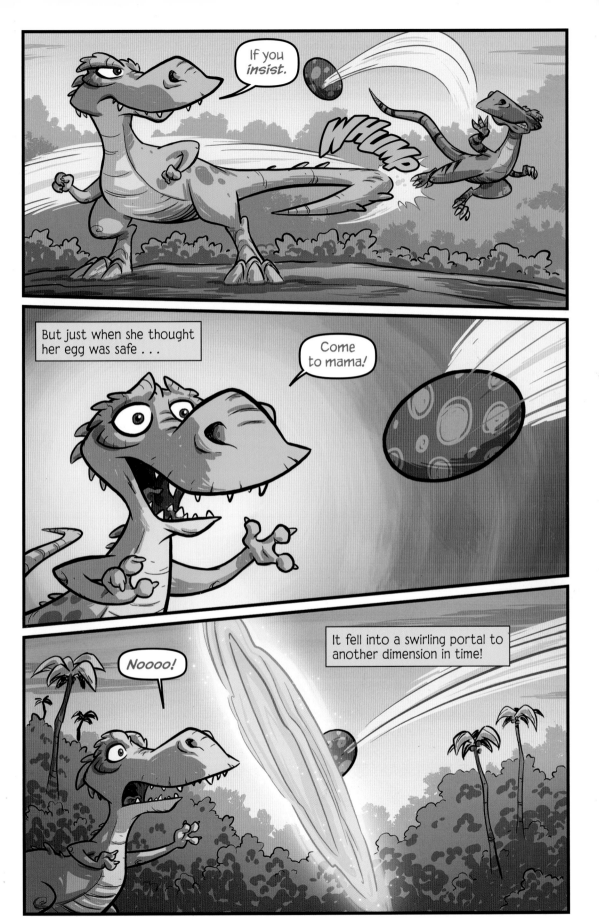

At first, Rex's strangeness wasn't a big deal.

Nighty-night, my babies.

But over time . . .

Come along, my babies!

You can do it, Rex!

His differences became harder to overlook.

BLUB
BLUB
BLUB

Almost impossible, actually.

Mother, I'm tired.

Hop on, my baby!

I'm coming on board too, Mama!

Aah!

Soon, Rex's duckling brothers stopped ignoring the differences.

The chicken crossed the road to get to the other side! Get it?

Ha ha!

ROARHOROAR! HOROAR!

Whoa. Turn it down, Rex!

I don't get it.

And ignored Rex instead.

Guys? Aren't we going to *play?*

Pretend you can't hear him.

Hear who?

Exactly!

They don't like me because I'm so ugly.

You're not ugly. You're just *different*.

What do you mean, *different*?

Fourth tried to explain.

There's an old saying...

If it *looks* like a duckling...

Swims like a duckling...

And *quacks* like a duckling...

Quack!

Then it's a *duckling*.

Rex raced to show his brothers what a good duckling he was now.

Wait, Rex!

Guys, look at me. I'm just like *you!*

The boys looked – then left as fast as they could.

Guys?

Wow. How embarrassing.

Is he joking with that get-up?

Not joking – just trying *way* too hard.

That night, when the ducklings thought Rex was asleep . . .

We took a vote.

You lost.

So you have to tell Rex he doesn't fit in here.

What?!

They're right. I *don't.*

16

19

22

Although Rex missed his duck family . . .

Good night, Fourth.

He stayed out on his own.

Good night, Rex...*wherever* you are.

But one night, something else returned to the pond . . .

Huh? What is *that?!*

The other animals came to investigate the mysterious object.

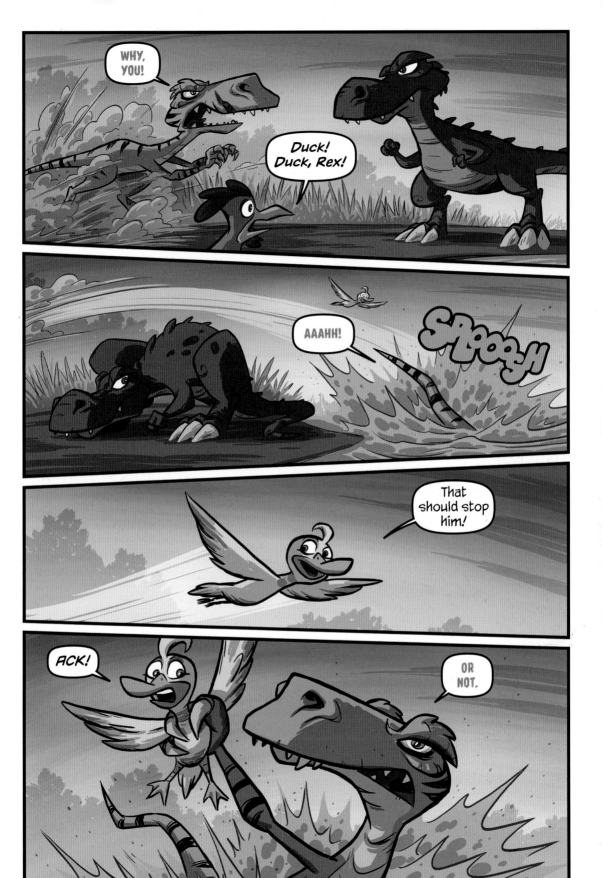

So Rex was transported far away to a different place in a different time. But every now and then . . .

He found his way back to where he first belonged.

ALL ABOUT FABLES

A fable is a short tale that teaches the reader a lesson about life, often with animal characters. At the end of a fable, there's almost always a moral (a fancy word for lesson) stated very clearly, so you don't miss it. Yes, fables can be a bit bossy. But luckily, they usually give pretty good advice. Read on to learn more about the original fable written by Danish author Hans Christian Andersen in 1843, and its moral. Can you spot any other lessons?

THE UGLY DUCKLING

One day, a swan egg rolls into a duck's nest. When all the eggs hatch, the baby swan - called a cygnet - looks a lot different from the ducklings. Although the cygnet swims better than his siblings, the farm animals tease him and call him ugly. Soon, even the mother duck says he doesn't belong. So the baby swan decides to run away. He tries living with wild ducks and then with an old lady and her pets. But he doesn't fit in. Out on his own, the cygnet nearly freezes during winter. In spring, the cygnet spots a flock of majestic swans. He worries they'll pick on him like everyone else has. But to his astonishment, they greet him with respect. Because he isn't an ugly duckling anymore. He's grown into the most beautiful swan in the entire pond.

THE MORAL

NEVER GIVE UP ON FINDING WHERE YOU BELONG
(In other words, don't change who
you are to fit in - find
where you're valued
for being YOU!)

A FAR OUT GUIDE TO THE FABLE'S JURASSIC TWISTS!

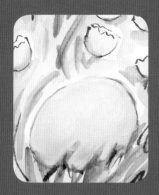 

The swan egg is swapped out for a dinosaur egg that has tumbled through a time portal!

In the original, even the mother duck and siblings teased the ugly duckling. Here, Fourth encourages Rex to stay true to himself.

The ugly duckling turns into a beautiful swan, but Rex grows up to use his awesome dino abilities to rescue the farm animals.

The swan leaves the ducks of the pond far behind. Rex still visits his duck family!

VISUAL QUESTIONS

The animals judge Rex because of how he looks. Do you think that's fair? Have you ever felt like you don't fit in? Talk about your answers.

The background in this panel is orange and yellow. Why do you think the illustrator chose to do this? What feeling does it create?

Rex is teased for being different, but his differences help to save the day. In your own words, discuss how Rex uses his unique dinosaur abilities to defeat the velociraptor.

4

List three ways Rex tries to fit in with the ducklings and farm animals. Did you think his plans would work? Why or why not?

5

THUD

THUD

THUD

Could it be?

The ground is shaking! The ground is shaking!

You think?

What is making the "Thud" sounds in the forest? How do you know that? Look back at page 26 if you need help.

The art in graphic novels can tell you a lot about what a character is feeling or thinking. How do you think Rex feels here? Use examples from the art and text to support your answer.

6

AUTHOR

Stephanie Peters worked as a children's book editor for ten years before she started writing books herself. She has since written forty books, including *Sleeping Beauty*, *Magic Master* and the New York Times best-seller *A Princess Primer: A Fairy Godmother's Guide to Being a Princess*. When not at her computer, Peters enjoys playing with her two children, going to the gym or working on home improvement projects with her patient and supportive husband, Daniel.

ILLUSTRATOR

Otis Frampton is a writer and artist. He is the creator of *Oddly Normal*, published by Image Comics. He is also one of the artists on the popular animated web series *How It Should Have Ended*.

GLOSSARY

decision act of making up your mind about what to do

eon long period of time that can't be measured

explore travel through a new area in order to learn or for adventure

familiar well known or easily recognized; if something *seems* familiar, you're not quite sure if you know it and can't fully remember

inherit receive something from a parent, such as looks, habits or skills

insist demand or ask in a very firm way

overlook ignore or not pay attention to something

portal large, impressive opening or entrance

poultry birds raised for their eggs and meat; chickens, turkeys, ducks and geese are poultry

precious having great importance or value

strut walk in a proud way

unique one of a kind and unlike anything else

wreck destroy or damage in a violent way

THE MORAL OF
THE STORY IS... EPIC!

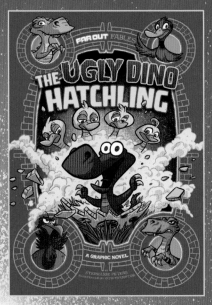

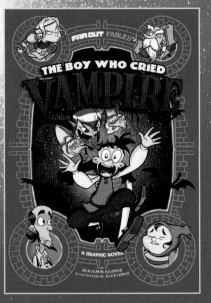

FAR OUT FABLES